# THE WORLD OF Dogs

# THE WORLD OF Dogs

## A. J. AND H. A. BARKER

### Exeter Books

NEW YORK

A Bison Book

PAGE 1: *Ruby Cavalier King Charles Spaniel. The Cavalier breed originated in England where it was crossed with other spaniels as well as with certain toy breeds imported from China and Japan.* PREVIOUS PAGE: *Two Maltese. The good-natured little Maltese is the oldest toy breed in the West. It probably takes its name not from the island of Malta, but from the Sicilian town of Melita. There is evidence that this breed was established in the Mediterranean area at the time of the Roman Empire and was a popular pet even then. It has changed little over the centuries.* THIS PAGE, left to right: *German Shepherd, German Long-haired Pointer, German Short-haired Pointer.*

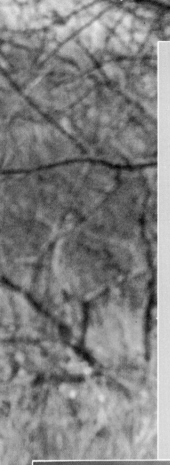

# Contents

# The First Dogs

For centuries, dogs have been part of the everyday life of people all over the world. Beloved by some, tolerated by others, and occasionally disliked, the dog is universally recognized as one of the most intelligent animals. Just how man and the creature which has been called his 'best friend' came to accept each other is a mystery. Originally they were enemies – rival hunters competing for similar foods – and up to the Stone Age period any kind of partnership between man and dog seems improbable. At that time the early dogs were akin to wolves, and prehistoric men and wolf-dogs were just as ready to eat each other as any other form of prey.

The domestication process took a long time, and we shall never know why or how it evolved. Perhaps the wolf-dogs prowled round man's encampments looking for opportunities to steal food or pick up a wandering child. Perhaps they were attracted by the bones and offal that men threw out of their caves, and these scraps forged a link between human and animal. In the course of the development of this relationship undoubtedly many dogs were killed. The first dogs were vicious brutes, but primitive men were equally vicious – wild creatures ready to defend their settlements against marauders with the same savagery they used in hunting. Nevertheless they had the rudimentary traits attributed to humans and, when dogs and orphaned puppies were caught, it was inevitable that some of them would be taken into the settlements. Having been reared by man, some of the puppies formed attachments with the people that fed them. Such dogs then began to identify themselves as members of the human family and their innate 'territorial' instinct led them to defend the territory of the humans that had adopted them against invaders – even their own species. With every succeeding generation of puppies born in the human settlements, the bond between man and dog grew stronger but the dogs retained their basic instincts. Primitive men feared darkness, for beyond the circle of light cast by the camp fire real and imaginary danger lurked wild animals and evil spirits, the latter no less worrying because of their immunity to attack. When it was realized that the settlement dogs were able to detect the approach of enemies long before human sentries noticed anything, they were put to work as guard dogs; through their highly developed sense of smell and hearing dogs could sense danger and raise the alarm. This enabled the men to prepare themselves for an attack. It was a short step from guarding man to guarding his other animals. As man acquired domestic animals the dog was called upon to protect them and to keep them together, that is, to act as a shepherd, and in the course of time the dog has been increasingly used in this role in the service of society.

The second basic instinct retained by the dogs born and bred in man's settlements was that of hunting. They no longer had to hunt for food, of course, since man provided that, but the natural instinct to chase and kill remained. Consequently, when early man found out that his dogs would cooperate in the hunt, they were employed in this role also and were used either to drive game in the direction of an ambush or to drag it down. Hunting in this manner went on for hundreds of years while succeeding generations of both men and dogs steadily became more and more domesticated and more familiar with each other's ways.

Undoubtedly the dog has changed considerably since the Stone Age days of the wolf-dog, and some people find it difficult to understand how so many different shapes and sizes have descended from one common ancestor. The answer is that, before today's multitude of breeds came to be recognized, a process of natural evolu-

*OPPOSITE: A Samoyed. The dog is a Spitz breed which takes its name from a Siberian tribe called the Samoyedes. It was introduced to the West considerably earlier than the other Arctic Spitz breed.*

tion in different parts of the world created dogs suitable for their own particular environment and conditions. This process, divergence in type, took millions of years, with mutations happening all the time. An animal which was born differing from the norm would find that this either helped or hindered him in his daily life. If the divergence was helpful, then those with the same abnormality would tend to thrive and breed in greater numbers, while those who found their mutation was a handicap would usually succumb in the struggle for survival and disappear. Thus the abnormal would become the normal until, in turn, the species took another step up on the ladder of evolution. The modern breeds of sight hound provide an excellent example of the evolution process. The original wolf-dog is believed to have been a comparatively slow animal, relying first and foremost on its sensitive nose and acute sense of hearing to find its prey, and then on its perseverence and stamina to track and eventually to catch it. On the plains and in desert country, however, speed was all important, for that was the only means of escape open to wild game pursued by its enemies. In such circumstances speed and sight were more important in the dog than the ability to detect by nose and ear. Thus a new type evolved – a rangy, long-legged, swift hunter from which are descended all the modern coursing dogs, such as the Borzoi, Greyhound, Saluki, Whippet, and Irish Wolfhound.

Primitive man would not, of course, have had any knowledge of the breeding processes inherent in the evolution of the dog. However, as the centuries rolled by, hunters and farmers would recognize that like bred like, and that a courageous dog mated to a brave bitch would usually produce puppies of a similar temperament. This would not always occur, owing to the interplay of genetical factors not understood at the time, but it was a good enough rule to ensure that breeders who required certain attributes in their dogs would stand a fair chance of success.

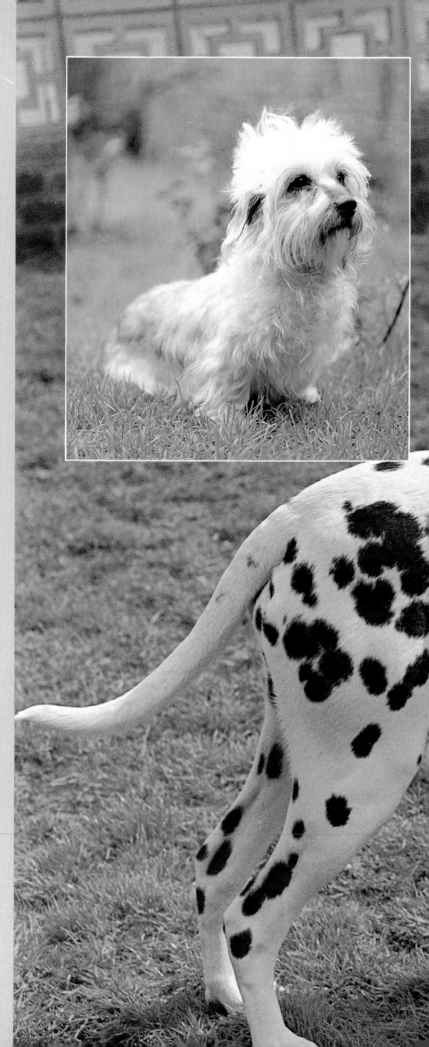

RIGHT: Dalmatian. The name Dalmatian implies that this breed comes from the Dalmatian coast of Yugoslavia, but various theories have been put forward that the dog originated in Denmark, Spain, Egypt or India. INSET: Dandie Dinmont. The Dandie Dinmont Terrier has a large following, especially in Britain.

Thus, by trial and error, a variety of dogs were produced – large dogs and small dogs, dogs with straight legs and dogs with crooked legs, dogs with thin coats and dogs with profuse coats – in effect, all the types of dogs which we have today.

Finally, with the passage of time, as knowledge grew, breeding became more scientific and dogs were bred for specific purposes – guard dogs, sheepdogs, hounds, pet dogs, handsome dogs, and grotesque dogs – in fact, every kind of dog for work, sport, or amusement.

*Bearded Collies. All Collies come from Scotland and the name derives from an old Anglo–Saxon word* Col, *meaning black. In Scotland the sheep were usually black in color and so were called 'Colleys.' The dogs that worked them were known simply as Colley Dogs. This eventually was shortened to 'Collies.'*

# Dogs in the Classics and in Legend

The Greeks and Romans loved dogs and writers and teachers of both nations wrote freely in praise of them. In Greek mythology, for example, Actaeon, a huntsman, surprised the moon goddess Diana while bathing, was changed by her into a stag and torn to pieces by his own hounds.

Geryon, another character in Greek mythology, was reputed to be a monster with three heads, whose oxen ate human flesh and were guarded by Orthos, a two-headed dog. In another Greek legend, Icarius, the King of Attica, was killed by men who had drunk his wine and concluded it was poisoned. Icarius' body was buried under a tree, and his daughter Erigone was directed to the spot by the howls of his dog Maera (the glistener). Erigone promptly hanged herself from the nearest tree and Icarius, Erigone, and the faithful Maera were all carried off to the heavens and changed into constellations – becoming the Wagoner, the Virgo, and the Canis Minor.

Another of the constellations is Orion, who in mythology was a giant hunter slain by Diana and who now roams the skies attended by his dogs Arctophomus (bear killer) and Ptoophagus (the glutton of Ptoon).

The Roman Emperor Hadrian is said to have ordered a State funeral for a dog as a reward for its lifetime of fidelity. This is a virtue for which dogs have been praised since ancient times, and one of the most famous examples is that of Argus, Ulysses' dog. This dog had been parted from his master for over 20 years and was very old

*OPPOSITE: Great Dane. This breed may have originated in Denmark, but there is no doubt that it was in Germany that the Great Dane reached its present standard of excellence. Its ancestors were the heavy Mastiff-type war dogs attached to Caesar's legions.*

when Ulysses, disguised as a beggar, returned to his palace in Troy. An old servant who had known Ulysses since childhood failed to recognize him but in the words of the *Odyssey*:

> Near to the gates . . .
> Argus the dog his ancient master knew,
> And, not unconscious of the voice and tread,
> Lifts to the sound his ears, and rears his head,
> He knew his Lord, he knew, and strove to meet;
> In vain he strove to crawl and kiss his feet:
> Yet all he could, his tail, his ears, his eyes
> Salute his Master and confess his joys.

Dragon, a dog owned by a certain Aubry of Montdidier, earned his place in legend for a different reason. In 1371 Aubry was murdered in the forest of Bondy near Paris. Nobody saw the murder, but suspicion fell on Richard of Macaire because a snarling Dragon flew at his throat. Richard, who was ordered by the judicial authorities to fight it out with the dog, was killed, and just before he died he confessed to the crime.

King Arthur is perhaps the best-known character in British mythology and his favorite hound was Cavall. Sir Tristam, one of the knights of Arthur's Round Table, whose exploits are recorded in Malory's *Morte d'Arthur*, is said to have had a dog called Hodain or Leon.

In Celtic mythology the foremost hero-figure was a mortal endowed with super-human faculties, Cú Chulainn. His name, which meant 'Hound of Chulann,' was given to him when he was seven years old after he had been compelled to kill the

guard dog of Chulann the smith. But Cú Chulainn loved dogs and his favorite was called Luath – a name which Robert Burns subsequently gave to his own favorite dog and to the poor man's dog representing the peasantry in his poem *The Twa Dogs*:

> A ploughman's collie,
> A rhyming, ranting, raving billie
> Wha for his friend and comrade had
>     him,
> And in his freaks had Luath ca'd
>     him
> After some dog in Highland sang
> Was made lang syne – Lord knows
>     how lang.

Fingal, the great Gaelic semimythological hero, whose name was given to the great cavern on Staffa which is supposed to have been his home, had a dog called Bran. And the favorite of Roderick, a Spanish hero around whom many legends have been collected, was called Theron.

Then there is the legend of the Mauthe dog – a ghostly black spaniel which for many years haunted Peel Castle on the Isle of Man. It was said to go into the guardroom at dusk and, while this specter dog was there, the soldiers dare not swear or mouth obscenities. This was because a drunken trooper had on one occasion uttered a string of oaths, lost his speech and died three days later. (Sir Walter Scott refers to this dog in his *Lay of the Last Minstrel*.)

*Beth Gelert*, or the Grave of a Greyhound, is a ballad by William Robert Spencer, recounting an old and widespread legend which, with variations, is found in Sanskrit and other ancient literature. Briefly, the story is that a Celtic chief Llewellyn, returning home from a day's hunting, is met by his favorite hound who is covered with blood. Llewellyn runs to see if anything has happened to his baby son, finds the cradle overturned and spattered with blood. Assuming the dog had attacked the child and eaten it, Llewellyn promptly stabs the hound to death. Afterward he finds the baby quite safe, and a huge wolf under the bed, dead.

Finally there is the tale of the *Dog of the Seven Sleepers*, Katmir, who, according to Moslem tradition, was admitted to heaven. (This was a special privilege, because dogs are generally disliked by Hindus and Moslems. One exception is made with the latter; the Arabs do not like dogs except for the Saluki, which is allowed to live in the tents and is bred with great care. An Arab cannot do any man a greater honor than by presenting him with the gift of a Saluki.)

*OPPOSITE: Dobermann Pinscher. The word 'pinscher' means terrier, and this dog was named after a German dogcatcher and breeder named Dobermann, who developed the breed. INSET: Dingo. This breed, native to Australia, is the only true wild breed remaining in the world.*

*ABOVE: These three Standard Poodles are groomed for a show. The two on the left are trimmed in the lion, or Continental clip. The one at the right is trimmed in the Dutch, or puppy clip. BELOW: Pointer. The Pointer is a gundog which searches for game.*

# Care and Training

Given proper attention a dog will remain healthy. The first consideration, however, is where the dog sleeps since this is a matter of paramount importance to him, is directly related to his comfort, and hence to his health. Even if he sleeps on the settee or on his master's bed, he should still have a bed or a sleeping place of his own where he can get away to snatch a quick nap. (The dog bed should be slightly bigger than the dog when it is curled up. A larger bed is not as comfortable to the dog as he likes to feel something around him while he is napping.) Dogs which are quartered outside need a snug and solid kennel which will give protection from the elements. It should be solidly constructed, however, with a windbreak at the door. Except in very cold climates, it should not be insulated. Insulation sometimes allows the humidity to build up, causing condensation to form, and this chills the dog making it susceptible to illness.

The kennel should face south (only in northern latitudes) and be slightly bigger than the dog when curled up; this permits its body heat to warm the kennel in cold weather. Finally, the kennel should be moved periodically. This not only keeps the area cleaner and allows the grass to regrow, but also helps to avoid parasite problems.

## EXERCISE

A pet dog should have some sort of exercise every day. A little dog can get exercise by chasing around the garden or by just being naturally active even in an apartment. A larger dog needs to be taken for a walk or allowed to run in a fenced-off area. Dogs which have insufficient exercise are apt to become fat, develop physical defects, and may even become neurotic. Letting a dog roam at will is not a good idea; not only is it dangerous for the dog, but such practice can cause trouble for the owner as well.

*OPPOSITE: American Cocker Spaniel—smaller than the British Cocker Spaniel, with a more profuse coat. BELOW: Labrador Retrievers. Some of the ancestors of this dog were Newfoundland dogs taken to Britain by Canadian fishermen who sold their catches in England.*

A dog that is tied up or confined to a run should have regular periods of free exercise out of the run. Whether it is work – such as training a hunting dog or herding cattle – or just a good run in the woods, the dog will appreciate it and will not become bored. A bored dog is often a barking dog.

## GENERAL CARE AND GROOMING

Care of a dog means keeping its teeth, coat, ears, eyes, and feet in good condition. Grooming is a matter of brushing and combing, clipping and stripping, shampooing and conditioning. Care and grooming go together, for if the dog is groomed regularly, many minor disorders of skin, eyes, teeth, or feet may be avoided completely, while others will be caught at an early stage when curing them is relatively simple.

### The coat

The dog's coat is the dog's complexion. A rich, full, and glossy coat means that it is healthy, while a dull, dry, lifeless coat which is constantly shedding hair means that something is wrong. Normally a dog's coat sheds out twice each year, in spring and autumn, although many dogs shed a little hair all the time. Excessive shedding between the shedding seasons may occur if the dog is not well, though many pet dogs kept in a house appear to shed continually. This may be because the house is too warm and too dry for the animal. Mixing a spoonful or two of fresh fat (bacon dripping, melted lard, or finely chopped suet) into the dog's food may help to limit the shedding. Sponging the coat with a weak vinegar and water mixture should also help. (Bathing the dog will *not* help, since baths tend to dry the skin and cause itching.)

In any event all dogs need regular grooming, not only to keep their coats looking good, but to keep oil in their hair and to remove dead hair. Moreover, grooming keeps the dog comfortable. Short-haired dogs are best groomed with a stiff brush and chamois cloth. Too stiff a brush should not be used or the dog's skin may be scratched. After brushing the coat thoroughly in the direction in which the hair grows, a chamois should be rubbed a

*RIGHT: Airedale Terrier. This breed is a descendant of the black and tan hunting terriers, now extinct, which were crossed with foxhounds in the Airedale Valley in Yorkshire, England. INSET: Alaskan Malamute.*

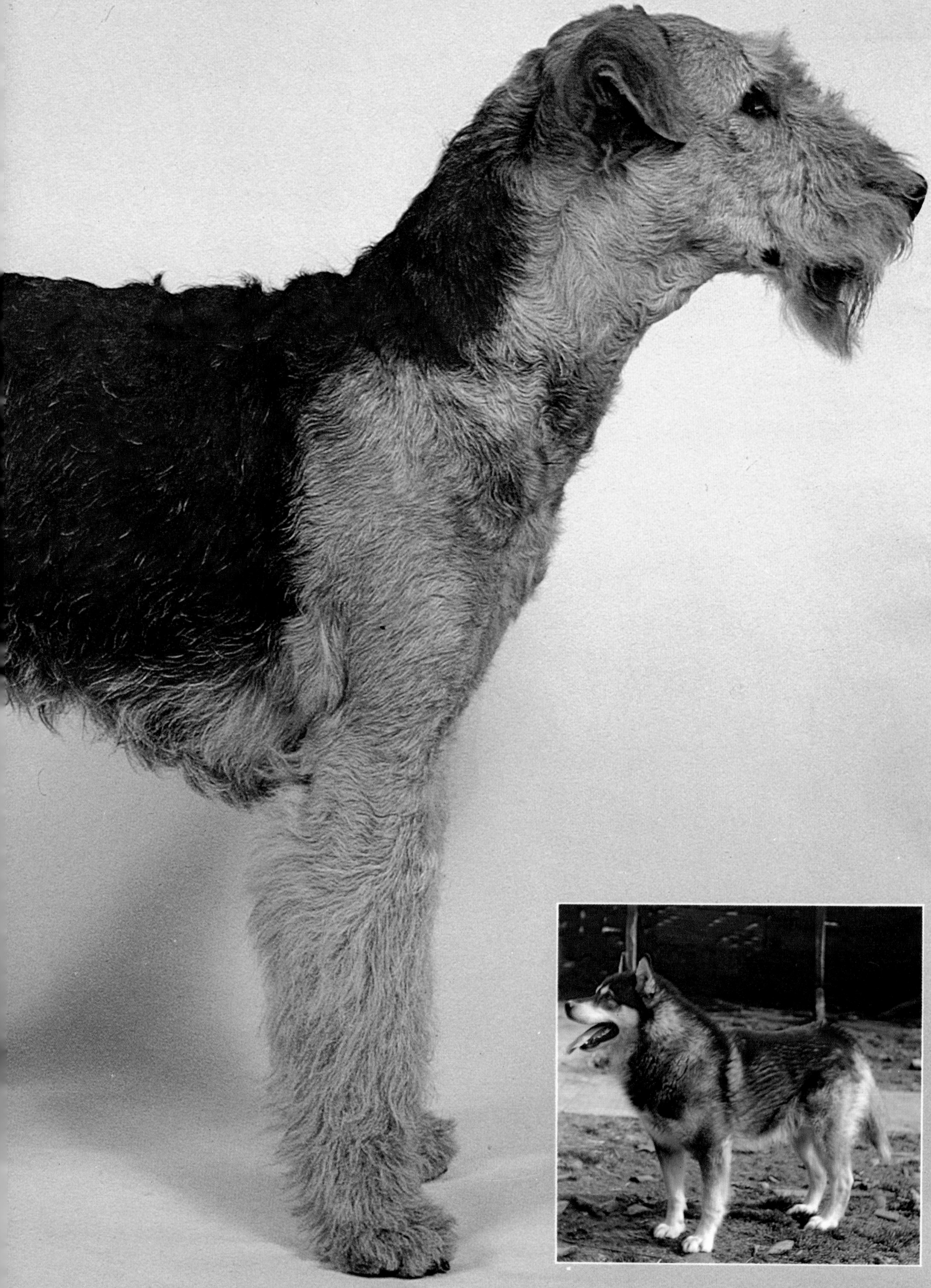

few times across it to add extra sheen to the coat. Thorough grooming of a short-haired dog, other than an occasional bath, takes only 15 minutes at most and will greatly improve the health of the dog's coat.

A medium-coated dog should be combed out first, or brushed with what is known in the United States as a 'slicker' (this is a flat brush with bent metal pins which is very effective for removing dead hair and stimulating the skin). Then the regular brush and chamois should be used.

Long-coated dogs such as Old English Sheepdogs and Afghan Hounds need more frequent grooming, first using a brush with straight metal pins, then a comb. Using a 'slicker' will tear hair out, and using the comb first will cause severe pulling if there are mats and tangles in the coat. Tangles should be eased out gently, holding the tuft close to the skin with the thumb and fore-fingers. Mats of tar can be removed by using an absorbent cotton pad soaked in acetone or a piece of ice. Burrs and teazles can be worked out with mineral oil, and the comb should be used only when necessary. The best tool is a brush.

The hair should be brushed every day, every single part of the head and body, legs and tail being brushed in the way the hair should lie. Thus, in the case of a smooth-haired dog, the hair should be brushed in the direction of growth to keep it trained down tight to the skin. Animals with stand-off type coats should be brushed against the grain to bring the hair up and away from the body. Long-coated breeds should always be groomed from the bottom of the legs upward to ensure that the coat

*Beagle. The Beagle is a hunting dog, used to track rabbits in most countries. But they are used to hunt leopards in some countries, such as Sri Lanka and Venezuela.*

is mat-free all the way through and not just on the top layer.

Finally, it is advisable to keep a careful watch while grooming for any fleas, ticks, or red, irritated areas. Taking prompt care of such problems will bring a faster cure and prevent further trouble.

## The teeth

Dogs seldom have dental problems other than those caused by disease or old age. They very rarely get cavities. The main trouble is decay caused by the feeding of soft food. A soft diet, consisting mainly of canned food or table scraps, does not keep the tartar cleaned from the teeth and as this builds up, it works down into the gum, often causing infection and soreness. A few hard dog biscuits or large bones to gnaw on will often prevent this trouble, as will keeping the dog on a diet of dry dog food.

Over and above the question of maintaining the correct diet, however, periodical cleaning of the dog's teeth is advisable. A mixture of one part of cold milk to three parts peroxide is suitable, as the milk cleans the enamel and keeps the teeth white, while the peroxide eradicates any decaying particles which have worked down into the gums. Clean the teeth using swabs of absorbent cotton or a baby's toothbrush.

Tartar deposits may be scraped off with a dental scaler, pressing the scaler gently down just below the edge of the gum until it is below the tartar, then scraping it off by pressing firmly against the tooth. It will help to swab with the milk and peroxide solution afterward. Heavy tartar deposits, however, are best removed by a vet, who should also examine the dog for any foul odor or redness in the mouth.

## The ears

The ears should be examined every time the dog is groomed. Not only do they frequently need cleaning – especially on long-eared dogs – but they are a favorite hiding place for ticks. Head shaking and hanging an ear down on one side are symptoms of pain, and a certain confirmation that there is trouble is an unpleasant smell coming from the ear. It is unwise for a novice to poke about in a dog's ear and, if trouble is suspected, it is best to consult a vet. Often it is just caused by the secretion of hard, brown wax, in which case a ball of absorbent cotton dipped in olive oil or liquid paraffin may be used to remove the lumps of wax. It is dangerous, however, for the inexperienced owner to use a probe in the ear, for if the dog jumps or the probing is too deep the eardrum may be punctured.

As a preventive for any form of canker in its early stages, dusting with boracic powder once a week should help to keep a dog out of trouble. But once trouble has started or been allowed to continue, then more qualified treatment is necessary.

Sometimes very tiny mites attack the ear and the dog is nearly driven mad with

*BELOW: Welsh Terrier. This breed is a sort of miniature Airedale, looking something like a Fox Terrier. RIGHT: West Highland White Terrier. Scotland has five main breeds of terriers—Cairns, Dandie Dinmonts, Skyes, Scottish Terriers and West Highland Whites.*

ABOVE: *A pack of English Foxhounds—smaller and with shorter legs than the American Foxhound.* LEFT: *An English Setter puppy.* INSET: *English Setter. One of the most attractive breeds of dog, the English Setter originated from English Hunting Spaniels.*

excessive irritation, and as a result is continually scratching the ear. In such cases no smell emanates from the ear.

It is absolutely essential when bathing a dog to plug his ears with absorbent cotton in order to prevent water seeping into the inner ear. So much ear trouble is caused by not taking this precaution. A single piece of cotton should be used in each ear, and if the point of the cotton to be inserted is smeared first with petroleum jelly, this will help to keep the ear even more waterproof. Needless to say, the plugs must be removed after the bath, otherwise they can work inward and cause trouble.

### The eyes

The expression of the normal dog is bright and intelligent, and when he is healthy his eyes are clear and clean. A change from the normal indicates that something is wrong. A staring, dazed expression with whites showing may mean overexcitement. Watery, weeping, or heavy lidded eyes may be a sign of an infection. This is not to say that all eye troubles are necessarily serious – weeping and discharge from the eye may simply be caused by a cold, a blow on the eyeball, or weed seeds lodged under the eyelids. Inflamed, red-lidded eyes,

however, merit the attention of the vet.

Weeping eyes should be attended without delay. Any mucus or scaly particles should be swabbed away from the corners of the eyes with absorbent cotton soaked in water to which a small quantity of Witch Hazel has been added. Many things can cause weeping eyes – foreign particles, inverted eyelashes, blocked tear ducts being the most common – and it is as well to find out the real cause from the vet before attempting any further treatment.

### The nose

To the dog the nose is more important than his eyes, although scenting ability differs with the breed. It seems to be keenest in those dogs which have a long nose, long ears, and hanging lips, such as the hounds and sporting breeds. Shape and color of the nostrils may also be important factors. The sharpest noses are generally those in which the nostrils are large, black, and open –

exceptions being the brown-nosed hunting dogs.

As the nose is also the organ of breathing, it works best when the nostrils are cool, clean, and free of mucus. (Incidentally, a cold nose as a sign of the healthy dog has been overrated.) A dry nose may be a sign of fever, although it is more often merely the result of a snooze in a warm place. A watering or mucous discharge, however, may indicate something serious. Such a discharge suggests distemper or a bronchial ailment, although it may also result from a simple cold. In any event, the nose should be cleaned with a soft cloth and the mucus in the nostrils removed with a swab; the nostrils should then be greased with petroleum jelly or olive oil to keep them soft.

## The feet

Another part of the dog's anatomy which needs regular and careful inspection is the feet. In many breeds, the hair between the pads on the underneath of the foot must be removed. This should be snipped away with a pair of small scissors; great care must be taken because it is easy to snip the pad. It is best to wash the feet first, soaking the pads and working between them with the fingers. This will remove any clots of dirt and, when the foot is dry, facilitate the snipping out of the hair.

Pads should also be regularly inspected for thorns, cuts, and cracks. Tiny stones will lodge between the pads, causing soreness if they are not noticed and removed at once. Tar is another problem, and often small lumps get embedded in the crevices of the pads when dogs are taken on tarred roads in very hot weather. They are difficult to remove and often a combination of soaking and cutting out is necessary.

Occasionally a dog may spend a lot of time biting and nibbling his feet, and the base of the nails will be seen to be in a slightly crusted, sore condition. In this case the vet should be consulted because the condition is usually caused by a fungus, rather similar to athlete's foot.

The dog's nails should be checked periodically. In most breeds nails are kept naturally short by exercise on hard surfaces and therefore need no cutting. Many house dogs, however, fail to wear

*RIGHT: Basenji. This dog cannot bark, merely yodel. INSET: Basset Hound. The Basset was used originally in France and Belgium for hunting deer, rabbits and hares. Later it was crossed with the Bloodhound.*

down their nails naturally and they can grow so long that they spiral until they stick into the pad. Such a condition is very painful and can lead to permanent damage if not quickly taken care of. The normal, well-worn-down nail is about even with the bottom pads of the foot, so that when the dog walks the nails just brush the ground. Nails should have a blunt appearance. When they begin to develop a hook, they are too long. A nail trimmer is a handy and inexpensive purchase and, with a little practice, almost anyone can keep their dog's nails trimmed and neat. When beginning, only a little bit should be taken from each nail. There is a vein that runs down the nail, and if the nail is clipped too short, it will bleed. Should this occur, a dab with a styptic pencil or a pinch of finely ground potassium permanganate crystals will quickly stem the bleeding.

### Special care for the aged dog

Older dogs often need special care to live out their lives in the best possible health. To begin with, the old dog cannot walk as fast or as far as he used to, so his exercise should be restricted; short walks at a more leisurely pace should be the order of the day, so that he does not get overtired. He will also want to sleep more, and should be allowed to do so – in a softer bed, warmer in winter, cooler in summer, because he feels the cold and the heat more in old age.

Teeth should be carefully watched as they wear down. Older dogs are often fed canned foods which do not remove the deposits of tartar that accumulate on the remaining teeth. These tartar deposits work into the gums, causing sore and inflamed gums, and then infection sets in. The teeth loosen and the dog is unable to eat at all.

The mouth should be checked periodically for irritation or redness. If there is any foul odor or sign of loose teeth, the dog should be taken to the vet for treatment before the condition becomes worse. All tartar accumulations should be removed as they form and not be allowed to build up to thick, irritating scales.

Deafness, which is quite usual in aged dogs, need not curb his activity but it may risk his safety. The first sign may be apparent inattention or disregard of words of command. The dog is not actually being disobedient – it is just that he cannot hear. To call him it will be necessary to tap on the ground to attract his attention or, if his eyesight is still good, to wave to him.

*BELOW: Bloodhounds. The Bloodhound's ancestors were French, although now it is considered to be a British breed.*
*RIGHT: Border Terrier. INSET: Border Collie. Both of these breeds originated in the Cheviot Hills in the border country of Scotland.*

Blindness is more serious than deafness in the old dog. As his sight fails he may well show signs of fear because he cannot see clearly. Not moving the furniture around and keeping things such as his bed, water bowl, and so on, in the usual places will ease his problems. This is even more important if he loses his sight completely. A dog which is totally blind can get around quite well and still enjoy life if a little extra care is taken.

## AILMENTS AND ACCIDENTS

### Abscesses

Abscesses are the result of a local infection and may appear on any part of the body. If possible they should be treated daily with a hot poultice. Ready-made poultices such as kaolin may be used; alternatively liquid garlic or witch-hazel should be heated and seaweed powder added to make a paste, which should be spread on lint. This should be applied to the affected part, and then covered with gauze and bandaged. The treatment should be continued until all the discharge has come away. If the abscess is in a difficult position where it is not feasible to apply a poultice, it should be treated with hot fomentations of salt water (one tablespoonful of salt to one cup of water). The dog's diet should also be watched and garlic tablets given three times a day.

### Anal glands

A dog has two small glands, one on either side of the rectum, called anal glands. These are scent glands and they empty into the rectum during a bowel movement or at times of fright. Unfortunately, the opening into the rectum sometimes becomes plugged with fecal material and does not allow the gland to empty. Thus the gland fills and can become infected. A dog with a full anal gland will drag its rear end on the ground or carpet in an attempt to squeeze this accumulation out of the gland. People used to think this meant the dog had worms, but this is not so. Worming a dog with infected anal glands can be dangerous, for constipation often goes along with the condition and, if the dog cannot get rid of the wormer, it may make it sick or even kill it. A vet can show you where the anal glands are and how to empty them yourself. If the glands are checked and emptied if necessary, they will not be so prone to infection. Feeding a diet of dry dog food or giving several hard dog biscuits daily will often help prevent the condition, as

RIGHT: *English Springer Spaniel, one of the eight different varieties of spaniel dogs.*
INSET: *English Toy Terrier.*

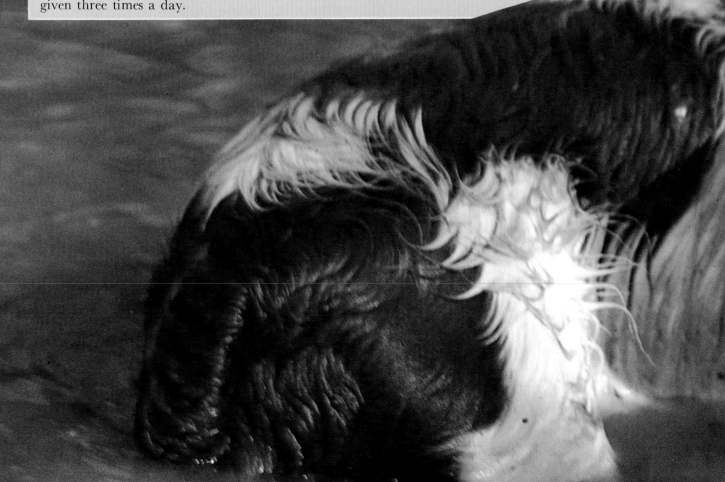

soft stools cannot empty the glands. Feeding a diet that will give a firm stool will aid the dog in emptying the glands naturally. Exercise will usually help too. In any event a dog should have the anal glands checked at least twice a year, smaller dogs about twice a month, since plugged anal glands can result in abscesses, lameness, and even hindquarter paralysis.

### Anemia
This is manifested by lack of pigmentation, that is, a pale nose. It is a dietary condition caused by lack of iron and can be rectified with a course of elderberry tablets.

### Appetite
If a dog is suffering from a lack of appetite, providing he is otherwise in good health he will regain his appetite if given a gastric mixture or gastric tablet before his meal and one wheatgerm capsule twice a day.

### Arthritis
Arthritis is often a problem with older dogs, especially with heavy, obese dogs. It is important that the old dog not be allowed to get fat. There is a tendency toward stiffness in old age, and the extra weight only intensifies the problem, making it crippling in many cases. Treatment with drugs, such as cortisone, aspirin, phenyl-butazone, and chlorphensin carbamate,

will often help dogs with periodic pain. Keeping the dog warm, in dry quarters, and off cement will aid in prevention of stiffness.

Often confused with arthritis, in older dogs especially, is lameness due to long or ingrown toenails. With less exercise, older dogs' nails do not wear down normally and require periodic trimming. If this is not done, the nails will grow, curl, twist, and even grow into the pad of the toe. This causes terrific pain, and the dog will be reluctant to move about; when it does so, it will limp badly. (see 'The Feet,' p. 234).

### Bad breath
This may be the result of incorrect feeding – especially tidbits. Clean the dog's mouth and teeth and give him daily garlic pills.

### Bites, cuts, and abrasions
Dogs suffer from the same kind of injuries as humans, including cuts, bruises, and scrapes; bites are more usually associated

*ABOVE: Borzoi. The Borzoi came to the West from the USSR, and until recently, was known as the Russian Wolfhound. It has a friendly temperament. RIGHT: Boston Terrier. During the nineteenth century Bulldogs were crossed with Terriers to produce the Boston Terrier, which was used in the cruel sport of dogfighting. It is a dog that is easy to train.*

with the animal world. However, the same type of first aid used for humans is indicated for these forms of dog injury. If the wound is minor it should be cleaned with liquid garlic or salt and water and then painted with iodine. However, if the cut or bite is a deep one, the bleeding may be stopped by putting a pad over the wound and applying pressure to stop the flow of blood until the vet's advice can be sought.

**Broken bones or fractures**

All too often these are a result of automobile accidents. When a dog has been struck by a vehicle the first two things to be feared are shock and internal bleeding. A broken leg or gash are minor worries when compared to these. Lift the dog gently on to a blanket or rug. On no account grab the animal around the waist or chest as this can push a broken rib through a lung.

Do not try to give the dog any food or water; an injured dog is usually in shock and is in no condition to take either.

Severe vomiting can result, which could start internal bleeding. Take the dog immediately to the vet. Often an injection of a clotting drug, stimulant, or immediate surgery can save the dog that would die otherwise.

**Bruises**

A bruise is bleeding under the skin and dogs sometimes get bruises just as humans do. However, a dog's skin is looser, allowing more bleeding, and the bruises fill with blood making a lump called a hematoma. They are often found on ears, due to flapping the ears in attempts to get rid of itching ear mites or dirt accumulation.

*FAR RIGHT, ABOVE: Standard Schnauzers. BELOW: Giant Schnauzers. RIGHT: Miniature Schnauzer. The name of these dogs comes from* schnauze, *German for snout or muzzle. The two smaller varieties are Germany's equivalent of the British terrier breeds. The forebears of the Giant Schnauzer were sheepdogs and cattledogs in South Bavaria that were mixed with other breeds.*

They are also often found on the neck from collar injuries, such as occur when a dog on a chain lunges forward. Bruises should be treated by a veterinarian.

## Burns and scalds

Needless to say, every effort should be made to avoid dogs acquiring burns or scalds in the first place. All fires should be well guarded and all hot cooking pans kept out of reach. Should the dog become burned or scalded, however, the affected parts should be dressed with an antiburn or boracic ointment, covered with absorbent cotton, and bandaged up. Subsequently the burn/scald should be dressed twice a day with ointment until it is healed. If the burn/scald is a sizable one, the vet should be consulted and the animal kept quiet as it will probably be suffering from shock.

## Coat

A dull coat, a thin coat, or 'staring' (lacking in body or sheen) may be a sign that the dog is out of condition or even that he has worms. If the coat is molting or thin, its condition may be improved by augmenting his diet with raw, red meat. Meantime a thorough daily grooming is essential.

## Constipation

A dog that is being fed incorrectly or not getting sufficient exercise may become constipated. Cure by dosing with castor oil or olive oil until the bowels recover. Plenty of exercise is very necessary.

## Cystitis

Cystitis is an inflammation of the bladder. It is quite common in dogs, but not always diagnosed, as many times there is just a mild inflammation which causes no visible problems. Cystitis is most frequently caused by bacterial infections and stones (calculi).

A dog with cystitis often urinates frequently, vomits, dribbles urine unconsciously, and appears to be restless. Lifting up the dog may bring yelps of pain. Often there is blood in the urine. Where the cystitis is caused by a stone, there may be a complete blockage of the urethra and the dog is not able to urinate. Consequently it absorbs the wastes, becomes toxic, and within a short time the dog is in serious trouble.

With an infection in the bladder, medication usually brings prompt relief, but the infection must be correctly diagnosed. Surgery is the best treatment for a dog with stones, as they are usually quite large and nearly impossible to dissolve.

## Diabetes

Diabetes is a disease that strikes dogs as well as people, and it most often occurs in fat dogs over four years of age. The first signs are an increased thirst and frequent urination, then there is a weight loss, quickly getting to the point of emaciation. In severe cases there is uncontrollable vomiting. When caught fairly early, and when there are no complicating factors, diabetes can be controlled quite easily if the owner is willing to spend a little extra time with the dog daily. As with humans, mild cases may be controlled by diet alone; the carbohydrate intake is severely cut, and the dog is fed foods such as lean meat, boiled eggs, and boiled fish. Other cases respond well to oral medication. Still other dogs need insulin injections daily, given before meals. The needle used is very small, and the injection is practically painless.

## Diarrhea

Diarrhea is nature's way of ridding the body of impurities and no attempt should be made to stop it unless it persists. The dog should then be fasted for 24 hours on honey and cold boiled water; it should also be given a mild laxative pill. Feeding should then commence with a white-meat diet.

If the diarrhea is persistent it could be a warning sign of more serious trouble – possibly coccidiosis, a disease caused by the parasite *Coccidia*. (Coccidiosis most often affects puppies, although adult dogs are often carriers and can affect young dogs. Damp, unsanitary conditions, and overcrowding help to spread the disease.) Dealing with this type of infection is beyond the capability of the normal dog owner and the vet should be called in.

## Distemper

Sometimes called the 'canine plague' because of its widespread occurrence and virulence, distemper is one of the most

*OPPOSITE: Old English Sheepdog. Sometimes called the 'Bobtail,' this breed is about 200 years old. It was originally a working dog used to protect herds of cattle from beasts of prey, but it has recently become more commonly a pet and companion.*

serious of all the diseases of dogs. The virus causing distemper is airborne and can affect dogs of any age, although it is most serious in puppies under a year old because such young dogs often do not have the strength to combat the disease.

The most common symptoms of distemper are: discharges from the nose and eyes; diarrhea and vomiting; an offensive odor from the skin, caused by slight skin eruptions; sneezing and coughing; loss of appetite; and sensitivity to light. Should an owner suspect his or her dog has distemper, the dog must not come into contact with other dogs, and the owner should avoid visiting other people with dogs since the disease is highly contagious. This is one instance where the vet should visit the owner – on no account should the dog be taken into a waiting room full of dogs. Treatment, once the disease has got under way, is often frustrating for both the owner and the vet. The sick dog may look better and show signs of recovery one day, but then get worse the next. Antibiotics will not cure the disease, as it is a virus, but they can prevent secondary infections such as pneumonia.

### Ear infections, Ear canker
Dogs, especially long-eared dogs, are prone to several types of ear infection. The most common is ear mites, which burrow into the ear, creating places for bacteria and fungi to enter. The moist, dirty ear that often accompanies the mites makes a perfect breeding place for these infections, and such bacterial and fungal infections cause considerable trouble. They often get a start from irritation due to dirt and wax accumulation, water or shampoo in the ear, foreign bodies, or injuries.

An infection can be suspected if the dog constantly scratches its ears with its hind feet, and rubs its head on the floor or against a chair. The dog may also shake its head, hold it to one side, and appear in pain. The inside of the ear is often red and swollen, may have a brownish, foul-smelling accumulation inside, and be hot.

Mild cases, caused by accumulation of wax and dirt, may be taken care of at home. An absorbent cotton swab should be dipped into methylated spirits and the ear swabbed out. The treatment should be repeated for two days. There should be a great improvement, but if not, the dog should be taken to the vet, for a severe canker is a task for him alone. Ear mites

are so tiny that they cannot be seen by the naked eye.

### Eclampsia
The most common form of this is the drying up of a bitch's milk. More often than not it is a small bitch with a fairly large litter that is affected. She will begin to pant, stumble, and fall when she attempts to walk and she may have convulsions. If not treated she will die.

The puppies should be taken from the bitch and handreared, and the bitch taken to the vet who will give her an intravenous injection of calcium. Most bitches respond rapidly, but they must be fed on plenty of raw, red meat.

### Eczema
In hot weather it is quite common for dogs to start scratching, biting, and licking themselves. Sometimes the remedy is to change to a white-meat diet; in any event the dog should get plenty of exercise. When the eczema progresses it causes bald patches, especially at the base of the tail and on the front feet. Irritation can be eased by swabbing the affected parts with methylated spirits or washing with a light disinfectant soap and then applying a skin balm. All the dog's drinking water should be boiled.

### Epilepsy, fits, and hysteria
Epilepsy is quite often seen in dogs, especially in some of the smaller breeds; Miniature and Toy Poodles and Cocker Spaniels are quite often affected. This is not to say many of these dogs have epilepsy, but only that it is more common in them than in Alsatians or Great Danes.

A dog with epilepsy will have recurrent 'fits' or convulsions. The dog shakes, stiffens out, falls, and jerks its legs; its head often tips backward. Excitement may trigger these seizures. They may occur only once a year or several times daily, and they do not last long. If the dog is running around, catch it and put it in a quiet and cool, darkened room. Then apply cold water compresses to the head. If the seizure persists, the vet should be

*Finnish Spitz. This dog (Suomenpystykorva in Finland) is virtually unknown outside of that country. But in Finland it is the most popular breed. It is kept both as a pet and as a hunter.*

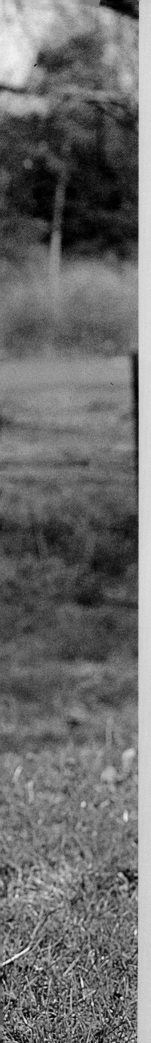

called in, for if epilepsy is diagnosed he can prescribe oral drugs which will usually keep the dog from having further seizures.

## Eyes

Inflamed and 'weeping' eyes should be treated immediately. The eyes should be bathed very gently with absorbent cotton swabs dipped in boric acid or sodium bicarbonate solution to remove any dirt or pus. A simple eye ointment like mercuric oxide should then be applied. Castor oil and cod-liver oil are old-fashioned eye soothers, and a drop of one or the other should be placed in each eye before the dog is taken out for a run in woods and fields. They help insure against the scratching and discomfort caused by dust, pollen, and weed seeds. Proprietary eye preparations for humans are excellent for dogs. There are also modern eye ointments which the veterinary may prescribe.

Inverted eyelids and in-growing eyelashes sometimes occur. These cause continual weeping and pawing of the eye and the vet should be called in.

## Fleas

When dog parasites are mentioned most people immediately think of fleas. In fact, fleas are a problem with very few dogs as long as a few preventive measures are taken.

Fleas are tiny, fast-moving, flat insects which suck blood and annoy dogs and people. Dog fleas will bite humans! Sandy, dry areas are favorite spots for fleas. They do not spend their life on the dog, but hop off and on. This is why, when treating the dog with a flea spray or powder, its bedding, rug, or sleeping place must also be treated.

If the dog does collect some fleas, groom it daily and apply an antiparasite powder, making sure it gets right down to the skin. Brush out one hour after applying. Bedding, baskets, and kennels should also be treated by dusting the powder well into the fiber or cracks in the woodwork. For an effective dip, see Ticks.

## Fungus infections

Fungus infections are often mistaken for mange by the layman. However, there are many types of fungus infections that can attack dogs, the most common producing bald, angry, red spots which appear either to itch intensely or to be very tender. Such spots usually occur on the neck and back and spread outward. The hair must be clipped from around the spot and the area treated with an antifungal ointment prescribed by the vet.

## Heart trouble

Old dogs, like old people, often develop heart trouble; overweight dogs are especially prone to it. Often the first signs that heart trouble is present are coughing and enlargement of the abdomen. A dog with heart trouble will often have poor circulation, with fluid settling out of the blood and into the tissue. This can often be controlled by use of diuretics, which stimulate the kidneys, drawing fluid out of the body. Salt intake should be restricted. There are also oral drugs, given to strengthen the heart, but these must be prescribed by the vet who will also advise on the dog's diet.

## Hepatitis

Hepatitis is caused by a virus and is therefore easily spread, often by the urine of infected dogs. Its symptoms resemble those of distemper. There is usually a fever, inflamed eyes, vomiting, no appetite, and diarrhea. The dog may develop white eyes, which can cause temporary blindness. This usually follows the acute period of the disease, where the dog is sickest; if it is not treated, it will usually disappear in a week or two. This condition is called 'blue eye.' The same condition sometimes sets in with distemper, continual weeping, or injury. It usually clears without treatment. However, the only safe means of prevention of hepatitis is to vaccinate susceptible dogs.

## Lice

Lice are tiny, slow-moving, grayish parasites which occasionally infect dogs. They do not move about like fleas but hook into the skin, hold fast, and suck blood. They are most often seen on medium-coated or long-coated breeds, as the long hair enables them to hide from the light. When lice are bothering a dog, the dog will usually begin to scratch excessively. On parting the hair it is possible to see the tiny lice and the little specks which are their eggs.

When lice are discovered on a dog, the entire dog should be clipped short. With

*OPPOSITE: Newfoundland. One authority has claimed that the Newfoundland is descended from Pyrenean Mountain Dogs (Great Pyrenees) taken to Newfoundland in the middle of the 17th century.*

no hair to hide in and protect them from an insecticide, the lice are usually easily taken care of. There should be a repeat treatment every week for three weeks to kill any new lice that have hatched out. The dog's bedding should be burned and its bed dusted with the same powder or spray as is used on the dog.

## Mange

Mange is quite common in dogs in some parts of the world. It is transmitted by tiny mites which cannot be seen with the naked eye (and which are often carried by humans on their skin!). The mange mites burrow into the dog's skin causing intense itching. Malnutrition accompanied by poor skin health often gives mites a start. Skin eruptions, especially about the face, legs, and belly, should be regarded as suspicious.

Pustules, scabby areas, thickened, grayish areas, and baldness are all symptoms of mange.

Mange is very contagious to other animals, so a dog suspected of having a mange infection should be isolated until it has been seen by a vet. Treatment entails completely clipping the dog and the use of medicated shampoos and special ointments which only the vet can prescribe.

## Obesity

Obesity is often due to incorrect feeding coupled with too little exercise and too many tidbits. A normal, balanced diet with a day's fast once a week and plenty of exercise should cure the condition in time.

## Rabies

Rabies is an infectious disease affecting many warm-blooded animals, including

man. (It used to be termed 'hydrophobia' because paralysis of the throat made it difficult for a rabid animal to drink.) It is more common in dogs than in any other animal, but it can affect and be transmitted by rodents, cattle, horses, cats, monkeys, and other animals.

There are two types of rabies: dumb rabies, in which the dog just sits, mouth often hanging open, and has a peculiar look in its eye, and furious rabies, when a dog has hallucinations, snaps at imaginary objects, is restless and irritable. Often, the dumb rabies is the more dangerous, as many people pry into the mouth, thinking the dog has something in its throat or mouth. Getting the dog's saliva into a small cut or scratch can give you rabies, so never try it. Not all rabid dogs, however, attack people and have frothy mouths. A rabid dog often has a personality change. A timid, fearful dog will become brave and friendly; a normally friendly dog will turn surly and timid. A rabid dog will often leave home and wander until exhausted.

There is no treatment for rabies once symptoms have developed in dog or man. Vaccination will provide protection, however.

*LEFT TO RIGHT: Miniature Bull Terrier, Bull Terrier, Cairn Terrier. The Bull Terrier was developed by the British for use in dogfighting. Bulldogs were crossed with Terriers. Other crosses were then made which gave the Bull Terrier its characteristic conformation and its more controllable temper. The Miniature Bull Terrier is merely a small-sized Bull Terrier. The Cairn Terrier was developed in Inverness, Scotland and is basically a pet.*

## Snake bites

A snake bite requires immediate first aid. Where the fangs have punctured the dog's skin the wound should be opened – with a knife, a nail-file, or similar instrument – and potassium permanganate crystals or damp Epsom salt should be sprinkled in. If there is a rapid swelling apply a tourniquet between the bite and the heart, loosening for a few seconds every few minutes. *Get the dog to a vet as soon as possible, for time is important.* (Most snakes are not venomous but the bites of nonvenomous ones can turn poisonous and so, for safety's sake, the punctures should be inspected and cleaned by a vet.)

## Stings

For a bee sting apply baking soda; for a wasp sting, liquid garlic; for a hornet sting apply alternatively a hot, then cold poultice of liquid garlic.

## Ticks

Ticks are blood-sucking parasites which dogs that roam woods and fields – especially near cattle – are apt to pick up. There are several types of ticks but all are basically the same.

In small numbers they generally cause no trouble except irritation. In large numbers, however, they can produce anemia and extreme agitation. Scratching and biting at the tick bites breaks off the tick heads, irritates the skin, and aggravates the dog's problem. Secondary infections often follow, and generally ticks can get into the ear canal, causing ear infections and irritation.

Ticks may be removed simply by pulling slowly but firmly. If they are yanked off, the mouth may be left behind to cause infection and soreness. Spots that look sore should be wiped with methylated spirits or iodine. Dips should be used regularly in tick-ridden areas, and flea-powder will also help. (An effective dip to kill ticks on the dog may be made with 4 oz of derris powder containing 3 to 5 percent of rotenone and 1 oz of flaked soap in a gallon of tepid water. For the dip the dog's eyes should be protected by applying petroleum jelly or oil around them. The same wash with half the amount of derris can be used for fleas.)

## Travel sickness

All foods should be withheld before a journey.

## Tumors

Breast tumors are sometimes seen on aged, unspayed bitches. They may or may not be malignant. With some tumors, injections of testosterone will result in regression of the growths. Spaying the female will also help in some cases. Surgery is recommended for dogs in good health, while the tumors are still small in size; if they are allowed to grow large, the chances of successful surgery are greatly reduced. Thus as soon as lumps on the breast are detected, they should be looked at by a vet.

## Worms

Several types of internal parasites – worms – may be harbored by dogs. They can be inherited but more commonly the worm larva is taken into the dog's organs through its food. The most common are roundworms, tapeworms, hookworms, whipworms, and headworms. (The latter is most common in the south of the United States and is usually fatal.)

Worms can sometimes be detected in the dog's excrement, but a microscopic examination is usually necessary to determine the type of worms present. External indication of the presence of worms include excessive appetite, laziness, loss of weight, eye excretions, and vomiting. These symptoms are common to other dog ailments, however, and therefore are not positive guides; only a microscopic investigation of the dog's stool can ascertain whether or not worms are present. Treatment for worms varies according to the types present and should not be undertaken without the advice of a vet.

## TRAINING

Training may be said to start with the education of the puppy, whose first lessons will necessarily be simple ones. To start with he needs to know his name and respond to it when called. The name itself should be short and crisp and pronounced clearly in a moderate tone of voice whenever the puppy is called. It will not take him long to connect his name with himself, especially if he is praised when he responds.

The next lesson is concerned with the

*RIGHT: Pekinese. It is estimated that this breed has been in existence for some 2000 years, having been developed as a miniature dog in China. In 1860, when the Summer Palace in Peking was sacked by the French and British, five dogs were taken to England.*

collar and leash. The puppy must first be familiarized with the wearing of a collar and, when he has learned to accept it, a lightweight leash or piece of string should be attached. The puppy should then be allowed to wander around, trailing the leash quite freely until he is familiar with that too. Then the real lesson starts. The owner should pick up the end of the leash and guide the puppy around the room. At first he may well resent the slight tugs at his neck which the guiding process entails, but he will soon come to disregard the tugging and accept that he is expected to go where his master leads him. As with all training, patience and understanding are the key factors.

Simplest of the puppy's early obedience lessons is persuading him to go to his bed. This merely entails him learning to understand that when he receives the command 'Bed' or 'Basket,' he is expected to go to his sleeping place. The association of the command with his bed can be strengthened by dropping one of his toys into the bed when the order is given. Eventually he will come to understand what is wanted but the owner may have to be persistent, as well as patient – and lavish with praise when the puppy shows signs of confusion.

In talking to a dog a friendly, conversational tone – not too loud and not too soft – should be used. A sharp, quick manner of speaking may be used for correction, while soft, slower tones are used for teaching. Address him clearly and distinctly, using as few words as possible and the same commands each time (for example, if 'Bed' is the order for him to retire, it should not be alternated with 'Basket'). Talk to the animal as you would to a child of limited understanding. When you say 'Ball' to a child and show him a ball, he learns to connect the sound with the object. A dog will do the same, and if this is kept up with a variety of objects, a dog will sometimes become so smart that certain words which you do not want him to latch on to may have to be spelled out.

Training a dog to 'Sit' and 'Stay' are important early lessons. Both commands are intended to curb the dog's activity, and 'Stay' is merely an extension of 'Sit.' The latter is taught during leash training and accomplished by a sharp pull on the leash and, if need be, by firmly pressing down his hindquarters until the dog assumes a sitting position. The 'Stay' exercise follows when the 'Sit' lesson has been learned. With the leash in the owner's left hand and the dog on the left, the right hand, palm flat, is brought up in front of the animal's face and he is told in a firm voice to 'Stay.' If he moves, the leash is given a short, sharp jerk to make him sit, and the command 'Stay' is repeated. The exercise is performed for only a few seconds at a time to begin with, then for longer, with the owner moving away and the leash going slack. If the dog gets up to follow, he should be taken back to the same spot and the lesson repeated. This exercise should be repeated with the dog standing up and lying down until the dog obeys the command every time.

For a dog to come when called is clearly important; if he is not taught to do so the dog will come when called only when he wants to, and one day he will refuse and perhaps end up under a truck. The lesson is best taught after the 'Sit-Stay' exercise has been mastered. A long length of cord should be attached to the collar and the dog ordered to 'Stay.' The owner then walks away from the dog to the end of the cord. Facing the pupil the owner then orders 'Come.' If the dog does not start forward, the owner can try slapping his knee as an added invitation. If he still refuses, a light tug on the cord should get him moving.

The 'Come-when-called' exercise should be practiced day after day until the dog responds to the command promptly, no matter how far he is let out on the cord. Later he should be tried off the leash in an area where he cannot run out into traffic. If he continues ignoring the command 'Come,' the owner should turn round and walk away. A dog that merely wants his master to play will be disappointed, change his mind, and return. If he does so, the owner should again be lavish with his praise. On no account should the dog be called to its master for disciplining; if the dog is to be scolded the owner should always go to the animal.

Training a dog to be clean about the house – house-training – generally starts when the puppy is between three and six months old (the actual age depends on

*OPPOSITE: Lhasa Apso. This dog is sometimes called the Tibetan Apso. It is a true Tibetan dog, and the Dalai Lama himself often presented them to high-ranking foreign visitors. Apso is the Tibetan word for goat.*

the size, type, and intelligence of the individual dog). The earlier one starts on the training, the more the pupil requires to relieve himself, and thus the teacher has to be ready to take the dog out more often. Everything, in fact, depends on how careful and alert the teacher is. House-training is a full-time job; a puppy simply cannot be trained in the morning and not in the afternoon, or trained for a few days and then left for a day or so. The object is to teach the dog to adapt to man's way of life. He is by nature a clean animal and with patience he will respond to the training very quickly.

By the time the training starts the puppy's master should have a reasonable idea of his dog's needs. At four or five months of age a puppy urinates and empties his bowel quite often. Cold, excitement, and con-fusion add to the number of times he needs to go and feeding almost always promotes the urge. This means that he will have to be taken outside the first thing in the morning and thereafter at two-hourly intervals. It is a good idea to watch the puppy's behavior just before he relieves himself; when he is about to urinate he rushes around sniffing the floor or the ground before squatting, and when about to defecate he generally turns round and round on a particular spot. These are sure indications and, as soon as he is seen to embark on these preliminaries in the house, it is best to pick him up, carry him out, and set him down to complete his business.

When the puppy is taken out he should be set down on the ground and, when he has relieved himself, he should be praised and petted and then taken in again. After his breakfast he should be taken out again. It is a good idea every time he is taken out to say 'Want to go out? Go out?' until the puppy associates the words 'Go out' with the need to relieve himself. And when he is taken out he should remain outside until

*RIGHT: French Bulldog. It is described as a miniature version of the British Bulldog. In 19th century Paris the French Bulldog became a sign of fashion. FAR RIGHT: Bouvier de Flanders. The Bouvier came from Belgium where it was used for herding cattle.*

something has been done. There will be mistakes, of course, until the animal learns to control his bladder and bowels; when he does make a mistake he must be corrected immediately. Correction should be limited to scolding, *never* a spanking, as the latter will merely frighten him. Puppies which are spanked while being house-trained will inevitably continue to make mistakes.

## Traffic

Like humans, dogs have to come to terms with the automobile. To ensure that a dog does not constitute a menace to itself or to others on the road, it must be either kept on a leash, or so well brought up and disciplined as to behave well at all times. (Many people do not appreciate that, if a dog causes an accident, its owner is held to be responsible for the damage, and this can be an expensive business.) The trouble is that roads and automobiles are alien to his nature and, although it is possible to train dogs to cope with traffic, very few are. In any event, according to a study conducted by a Viennese vet who observed the behavior in traffic of 400 dogs, very few canines are fit to run off the leash. Those that did behave well were police dogs and guides for blind people – big dogs which had had a long, specialized, and intensive training.

*LEFT ABOVE: Long-haired Dachshund. LEFT BELOW: Wire-haired Dachshund. ABOVE: Smooth-haired Dachshund. Dachshund in German means 'Badger Dog,' and is one of the most popular breeds. There are six varieties: standard and miniature sizes in Long-haired, Smooth-haired and Wire-haired.*

## The dog in the automobile

Today's dog travels a lot in an automobile, and for some canines there is no greater pleasure than being driven around. Other dogs cannot tolerate automobiles. They become sick and nervous, wanting to be out of the vehicle and generally making the journey miserable for the other passengers. In the majority of cases the answer to this problem is training. This should be initiated when the dog is a puppy. Short drives will get him used to the motion of the vehicle, and giving him no food or water for at least two hours before a journey should help him to overcome automobile sickness. A passenger holding him on his or her lap, or sitting him on the seat beside him/her, will help to give him confidence. Letting the dog see out of the window also helps and discourages sickness, but he should not be allowed to lean out of the window as the rush of air may cause cold in his eyes and ears.

On no account should the dog be forced into the automobile while he is being taught to accept it. If he is afraid he should be put into the vehicle for a short time while it is stationary; gradually he will become accustomed to it and can be taken for a short drive. If, during the period of trial runs, the dog becomes uneasy, it is best to stop and let him out of the vehicle, taking him for a short walk before driving him home again. Most dogs gradually become used to the idea and become travel enthusiasts. For those who are less enthusiastic and who get excited and sick, the vet can prescribe drugs which have a soporific effect.

The trunk is no place to carry a dog; he will be confined in a dark, restricted space, and during the journey he may swallow dust, lethal exhaust gases, and gasoline fumes. As the trunks of most cars are located close to the rear axle, the wretched animal will also feel every bump in the road.

Leaving a dog in a parked automobile in the sun with the windows closed is equally as callous as transporting it in the trunk. If the dog has to be left in the automobile, the vehicle should be parked in the shade with the windows lowered a few inches on either side. If he has been kept on a leash, this should be removed to ensure he does not strangle himself, and, if the owner is to be gone any length of time, a bowl of water should always be left on the floor.

It is perhaps unnecessary to remind the reader that, if one takes a dog on a long journey, he must be given an opportunity to run around three or four times a day and to perform his natural functions. (Needless to say, special care has to be taken if the dog exercises near a busy road.) Finally, a light diet is recommended for a long journey: dog biscuits and canned food are probably the most convenient form, and plenty of water should be made available when the meal is given – especially in hot weather.

## Dogs and television

For humans television is now an established facet of modern life, and in the United States the dog-food industry has financed television programs for dogs. Their value is debatable but it can be argued that big business rarely sinks money into publicity ventures which will not show any return.

For many years a specific point was made that dogs cannot recognize moving pictures. However, an American scientist has claimed to have proved that dogs' mouths actually watered when the animals under test were shown a film of other dogs being fed. In all probability the reason for this was that the appearance of the dogs on the screen was combined with barking and yelping—noises to which any normal dog will react. So far as television is concerned, dogs may be classified either as 'curious,' who become addicts, or 'uninterested,' to whom the small screen holds no attraction.

## Travelling with dogs

Travelling with a dog inevitably creates problems. In recent years hotels have become more disposed toward dogs but, before undertaking a journey which includes a stay at a hotel, it is advisable to determine whether dogs are welcome.

As a general rule the smarter (and more expensive) the hotel, the more likely it is to accept dogs on the grounds that the guest is king and kings are expected to have an entourage. However, the entourage is expected to behave with decorum, and to take consideration of other guests. Thus a dog can only be left on his own in a hotel room if, in the absence of his owner, he does not bark or howl – or vent his feelings on the furniture.

Some hotels will supply dog food, but it is as well to remember that nothing is more detrimental to the dog's digestive system than strongly spiced hotel leftovers. The charges for accommodating dogs are usually based on size and whether or not food is provided.

Before one gets to the hotel, however, there is the journey. Travel by automobile has already been covered; the alternatives are the railroad and airplane. By train the dog usually travels in the guard's van in many countries, and he has generally to be accommodated in a closed (and ventilated) box which has been clearly labelled with the name and address of the owner, and the animal's destination. Before the journey it is desirable to let the dog sleep a couple of nights in this box in order to get him used to the idea of being cooped up; in the box he should have his own familiar blanket.

In an airplane the dog travels in the air-conditioned section of the plane's hold, in a special dog box with water and food. At stops en route the owner can not normally see his pet, but on long journeys overseas the ground staff – who are responsible for seeing the dog is comfortable and exercised – are often happy to relax this rule. It is perhaps unnecessary to mention that there are special rules governing the movement of animals from one country to another. Britain, for example, requires an imported dog to spend six months in quarantine, and the minimum requirements elsewhere are certificates of good health and vaccination.

*RIGHT: Long-coat Chihuahua. FAR RIGHT: Smooth-coat Chihuahua. These are the two types of this dog that is named after the Mexican state and city of Chihuahua. The Smooth-coat, however, may be the true Mexican breed.*

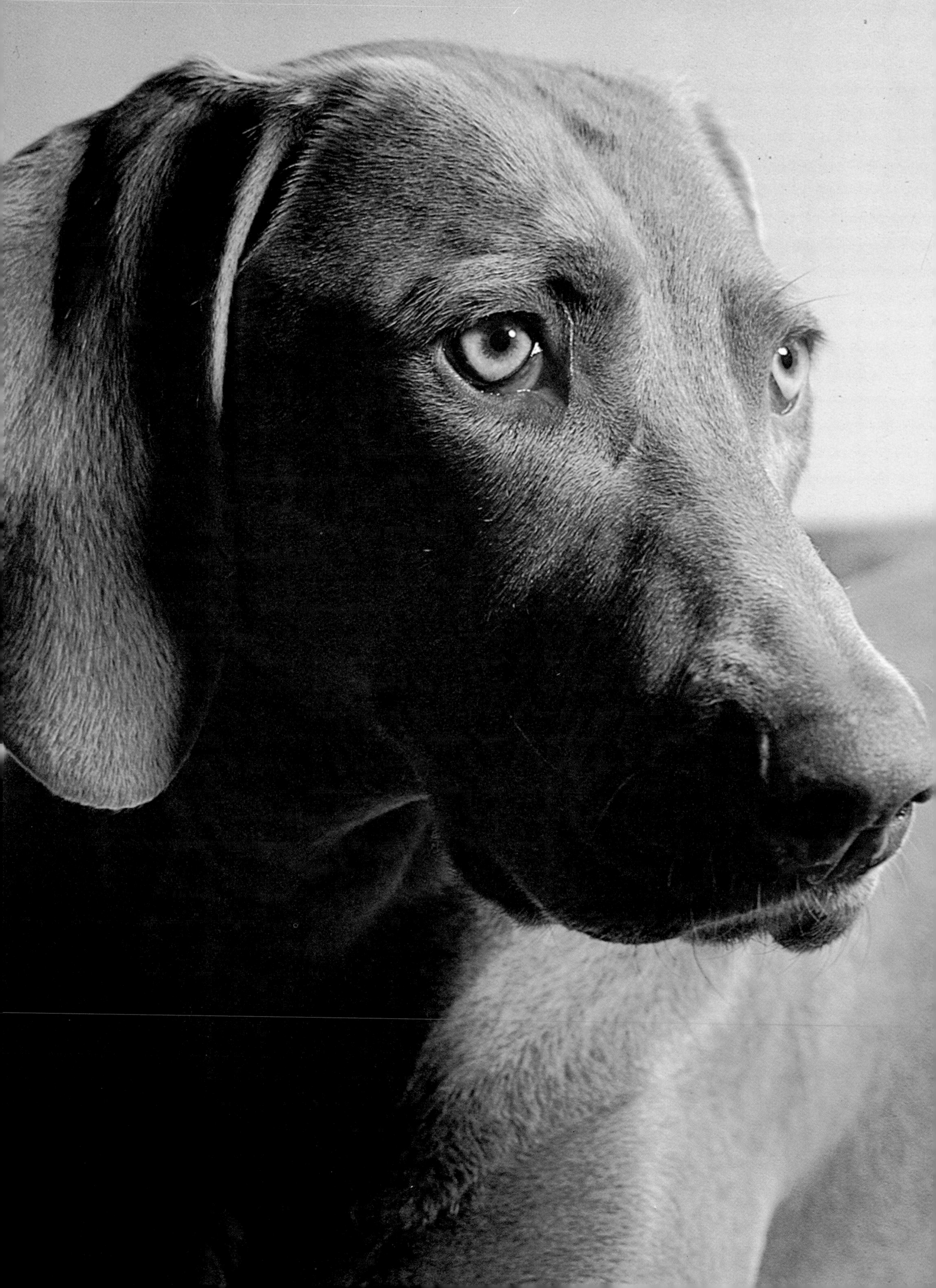

## Fat dogs and fat people

As a footnote to this chapter comes a recommendation that owners who have fat dogs should watch their own weight. United States' vets say that obesity is a major health problem for America's millions of pet dogs. By one estimate, 28 percent of the domestic dog population a decade ago were overweight. More recently it has been estimated that 30 to 60 percent of all pet dogs are obese, with the health of 20 percent of those in imminent danger. The main reason: mismanagement by pet owners.

America's 45 million dogs and 25 million cats can do little about the quality or quantity of food they eat. Many dogs will eat relatively unpalatable things simply as part of a social interaction with their masters. And obesity overloads the various systems of the animal, creating much more work for the heart. Dogs in the wild travelled in packs and lived in a feast or famine situation. As a result they have a survival instinct that involves a sense of not knowing where their next meal is coming from. Boredom can also be a factor. In any event the studies in the United States indicate that overweight dogs tend to be owned by overweight people. Americans spent $2000 million on pet foods in 1978, nearly three times the $725 million spent in 1969, according to the Pet Food Institute, a trade association. To stay healthy, dogs must be properly fed, as much harm and illness is caused by incorrect feeding, not only the type of food but when and how it is given. In their natural surroundings in the wild, dogs would hunt and kill their prey and eat its raw flesh, including the intestines, stomach contents, and bones. They would drink from streams and ponds and seek out wild fruits and grasses with which to satisfy their nutritional needs and balance their diet. The modern, 'civilized' dog cannot do this; he is wholly dependent on his master/mistress and, although a mature dog can live on a wide variety of diets, many of these will not keep him in the best of health; a poor diet may even shorten his life by several years. A growing puppy is even less able to stand a poor diet.

A correct diet is based on the natural foods which dogs would seek out if they lived the way nature intended. Protein is the most important nutrient. However, if the diet is to be correctly balanced, a certain amount of vitamins and minerals must also be present as well as sufficient carbohydrates and fats. Protein is needed for body growth and maintenance. It gives energy and is also frequently combined with fatty acids; these fatty acids are needed for a good skin and coat. Carbohydrates mostly produce energy, and fiber is also needed for efficient digestion. Of the minerals that are needed for good health, it is sufficient to mention calcium and

*BELOW: Field Spaniel. The Field Spaniel shares the ancestry of the other Spaniel breeds, but has remained a working breed and is normally seen at field trials rather than at formal dog shows.*

*LEFT: The Weimaraner has an excellent nose and is useful for both tracking and retrieving.*

phosphorus which are required for the teeth and bones; iron, copper, and cobalt are needed for healthy red blood cells.

Translating these requirements into practical terms, it follows that – as with humans – fresh food is best. The main constituent of the dog's meal should be meat. This should be fed raw, for if it is cooked it loses a lot of its goodness and the food is broken down so that the dog's teeth and its digestive system have little work to do, with the result that the latter deteriorates. (For this reason no minced, soft, or sloppy foods should normally be included in the diet.)

Good dog meat is expensive and fortunately there are a number of alternatives to lean, red meat. Ox cheek, heart, and raw tripe all have good nutritional value, and fish can be substituted for meat one or two days a week. Liver is also a meat but it should be given only once or twice a week. Offal, such as heart, lights or kidney, can be given occasionally but they should be cooked. White meats, such as chicken or rabbit, are useful alternatives in corrective diets, that is, when the dog is unwell. Raw meat should be given in large chunks, and all the bones should be removed from chicken or rabbit; fish should have the bones taken out after cooking.

A certain amount of green vegetables must supplement the meat. These should be chopped small and fed raw. Parsley and watercress are best since these contain iron and vitamins A and C. Other suitable vegetables are spinach and cabbage; root vegetables other than carrots are not suitable. Carrots, however, are good for dogs – either grated into the meat dish or given to the animal to gnaw. 'Roughage' is also an essential part of the diet, and lack of roughage is responsible for a lot of anal gland trouble. In a natural raw diet roughage can consist of wholemeal biscuits, or wholemeal bread baked or toasted and cut into biscuit-sized pieces.

Contrary to popular belief that they bring sheen to a dog's coat, eggs are not especially good for dogs. The only time they really are beneficial is when an animal needs extra protein, that is, after an illness or for a stud dog. The yolks of eggs may be fed raw, but uncooked white of egg destroys an important vitamin, biotin, in the intestines. Whole eggs generally should be cooked.

The majority of dogs like bones and in many cases bones are good for the animals –

*RIGHT AND BELOW: Bulldogs. In the 14th century these dogs were used in the cruel sport of bullbaiting. They were trained to seize the bull by the nose and not to let go until the bull fell and the fight ended. BOTTOM: Bullmastiff. The heavy and powerful Bullmastiff is believed to be the result of crossbreeding Bulldogs with Mastiffs. They are used as guard dogs.*

exercising their jaws and internal muscles, and promoting the gastric juices. But in some instances bones are definitely bad. It is really a matter of how the dog tackles the bone. The gnawing type is all right; he will just gnaw away for hours and no harm will be done. However, if he is a bone 'chewer,' then bones are not for him. This is the type of dog that gets hold of the bone between his jaws and crunches away, breaking pieces off. Then, if these are swallowed, they can cause a blockage in the stomach, or if they are sharp pieces they may puncture the intestines. In any event the only kind of bone to give to a dog is the large marrow bone; for small dogs such marrow bones may be cut in half. Chicken, rabbit, chop, or any other type of bone that is likely to splinter should *never* be given.

One good fresh meat or fish meal a day is sufficient for the average dog as a mature animal can eat a full day's food at one go. Kennel owners usually feed their dogs once a day – usually in the evening – and this is not a bad rule for the family dog. With older dogs (12 years old or more perhaps) the meat meal could be divided, half being given at midday and the other half in the evening. A further roughage meal of wholemeal biscuits or baked wholemeal bread can be given either three hours before or three hours after the meat meal. (The three-hour interval is important to the digestive system.)

As an alternative to separate fresh foods, there are ready-to-eat foods. Fresh foods have to be prepared, mixed, and sometimes cooked; ready-to-serve foods come out of a package or can and many dog owners consider that this is the easiest and most economical way of feeding their dogs. Most well-known brands of ready-to-eat foods provide a completely balanced diet, and the main advantage in serving them is that little work is involved and the dog is unlikely to suffer from the digestive upsets which are common in dogs that are shifted

*OPPOSITE: Silver Standard Poodle and Miniature Poodle. The Standard Poodle was once used as a gun dog. ABOVE: Siberian Husky. This dog is comparatively more 'civilized' than other Arctic Spitz breeds.*

from one kind of food to another when only left-over table scraps are fed. Regretably many dog owners feed their animals only on table scraps and the danger is that such dogs will get mostly carbohydrates and fat trimmings that have few vitamins, little protein, and not enough minerals.

Dogs should never be given tidbits. In particular they should not be given any highly spiced, fried, or greasy foods, or foods with sharp 'edges.' (As an example, feeding French fries to a dog can be dangerous. Some dogs do not chew their food and, when unchewed French fries reach the stomach, the sharp edges and points can cause such pain that the dog can actually be thrown into convulsions.) Provided the correct quantities are offered, the two meals suggested (one main meal and one roughage) should be ample to maintain the dog in good condition. The average dog, given free choice, will not overeat and will stay in just the right shape so long as it gets some regular exercise.

Whenever possible the dog should be fed at the same time and in the same place every day. Dogs are creatures of habit and they enjoy regularity; this will also keep appetites steady and bowel movement regular. Fresh, cool water should be available to drink. Milk should not be given to an adult dog because it is acid forming, and the only time it is beneficial is when the dog has been ill. After a reasonable time any food not eaten at the meal should be taken away. At the next feeding a little less should be offered until there is no food left at feeding time and the dog has eaten enough. Moist food such as dry food mixed with liquid or canned food should never be left in the dish and accessible; it can become sour or have a high bacterial growth, and the dog may be ill if it should eat the food later in the day.

It is important for the dog's food to be mixed fresh each time. It should not be kept standing until it becomes unappetizing, nor should it be served hot or chilled. Ready-to-eat dry dog food should be kept in a cool, dry place, protected from flies and other insects. Canned dog food, after it has been opened, should be kept in the refrigerator.

There will be occasions when a dog will sniff at his dinner or take a brief nibble or two and then walk away. This is no cause for alarm; this is the dog's way of giving his stomach a rest. When he has done so his appetite will return. Meantime the food

should be taken away and a fresh dish prepared and served at the next regular mealtime. Similarly, there is no need for alarm when a dog regurgitates undigested food, for it usually means that he has eaten too quickly and the digestive juices have not started to flow sufficiently to cope with the sudden intake of food. Many people worry when their dogs 'wolf' food, but a dog's digestion does not start in its mouth as it does in humans. Eating fast and swallowing food whole is natural for a dog and is probably a hangover from the time when dogs ran with a pack and had to grab their share or go hungry.

Finally, the accompanying charts provide a general guide to the feeding of adult dogs and puppies. When relating the quantities of food recommended in the two charts the following points should be borne in mind:

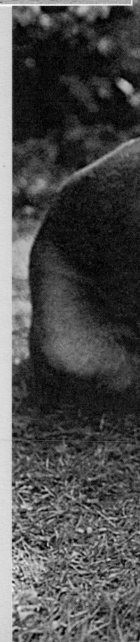

*ABOVE: Braque d'Auvergne. This breed is a hunter. RIGHT: Boxer. It is friendly and even playful. FAR RIGHT ABOVE: Braque St Germain. It is thought that this dog originated as a cross between an English Pointer with a French Braque early in the 19th century.*

## FEEDING CHART FOR ADULT DOGS

| Size of breed | Calories per day | Number of feedings | Raw meat or fish (cooked)* | Biscuits or wholemeal *Amount per feeding, mixed, moistened with water, milk, or meat broth* | Canned dog food (alternative) *Amount per feeding, mixed, moistened with water, milk, or meat broth* |
|---|---|---|---|---|---|
| Very small *Averaging 5–15 lb* | 250–600 | I | 3–4 oz | ½–1½ cups (UK) ½–1¾ cups (USA) | 2–4 tbsp |
| Small *Averaging 15–30 lb* | 600–1200 | I | 4–6 oz | 1½–2½ cups (UK) 1¾–3 cups (USA) | ½–¾ cup (UK) ½–1 cup (USA) |
| Medium *Averaging 30–50 lb* | 1000–1600 | I | 6–9 oz | 2–3¼ cups (UK) 2½–4 cups (USA) | ¾–1¼ cups (UK) 1–1½ cups (USA) |
| Large *Averaging 50–80 lb* | 1500–2500 | I | 1–1½ lb | 3–5 cups (UK) 3¾–6¼ cups (USA) | 1¼–2 cups (UK) 1½–2½ cups (USA) |
| Very large *Averaging 100–175 lb* | 3000–5400 | I | 1½–2 lb | 6–11 cups (UK) 7½–13¾ cups (USA) | 2–4 cups (UK) 2½–5 cups (USA) |

*\* If fresh, raw meat is given, the meat should be supplemented with vegetables*

## FEEDING CHART FOR PUPPIES

| Size of breed | Calories per day | Number of feedings | Raw meat | Dog meal *Quantity per feeding, mixed, and moistened thoroughly with whole (preferably) or evaporated milk* | Canned dog food *Quantity per feeding, mixed, and moistened thoroughly with whole (preferably) or evaporated milk* |
|---|---|---|---|---|---|
| Very small *Puppy weight 1–2½ lb* | 100–300 | 4 | 1–1½ oz | 1–3 tbsp | 1–3 tbsp |
| Small *Puppy weight 3–7 lb* | 300–600 | 4 | 1½–3 oz | ⅛–¼ cup (UK) ⅙–⅓ cup (USA) | ⅛–¼ cup (UK) ⅙–⅓ cup (USA) |
| Medium *Puppy weight 6–12 lb* | 600–900 | 4 | 3–4 oz | ¼–½ cup (UK) ⅓–⅝ cup (USA) | ¼–½ cup (UK) ⅓–⅝ cup (USA) |
| Large *Puppy weight 10–15 lb* | 800–1200 | 4 | 4–6 oz | ½–¾ cup (UK) ⅝–1 cup (USA) | ½–¾ cup (UK) ⅝–1 cup (USA) |
| Very large *Puppy weight 15–25 lb* | 1000–2000 | 4 | 6–8 oz | ½–1 cup (UK) ⅝–1¼ cups (USA) | ½–1 cup (UK) ⅝–1¼ cups (USA) |

1. If dry or canned food is being used, it is always a good idea to follow the manufacturer's feeding instructions. However, these are for the 'average' dog, and many small, active dogs eat almost as much as a big dog which spends its time lying around snoozing. It will therefore be necessary to determine a particular dog's food requirements by trial and error.

2. This is a continuing process. It is necessary to watch to see how much food the dog will eat readily, and whether he gains or loses weight. Some dogs get fat because their owners continue to give them the same quantities of food as they were getting when they were lively, active, and growing puppies.

3. Puppies actually need about twice as much food for their weight as do adult dogs.

The needs and appetites of individual puppies vary considerably, so their intake may need to be varied according to their size and temperament. However, from the time they are weaned until they are four weeks old, all puppies should be kept on a milk diet and light gruel. (It is best to use cow's or goat's milk, *not* dried or canned milk.)

From four weeks to two months the puppies should have *five* meals daily at three-hourly intervals starting at, say, 8 am. On this basis the main meal is given at 2 pm: see the chart for puppy feeding for quantities. The other meals should consist of cereal – wheat flakes, corn flakes, and so on (about 1–2 oz for medium, 2–3 oz for large, and 3–5 oz for very large breeds).

From two to five months the puppy should have *four* meals daily. These meals are similar in content to those given up to two months, but the quantities of the cereal-milk/water mixture are increased (very small and small breeds 1–3 oz, medium 2–3 oz, large 4–6 oz, and very large breeds 6–8 oz). For the final meal of the day puppy-size wholemeal biscuits can be offered. As before, the main meal should be taken toward the middle of the day and the quantities of raw meat offered are: very small and small breeds 1–3 oz, medium 3 oz, large 4–6 oz, very large 6–8 oz.

Between five and nine months of age the puppy is reduced to *three* meals per day, with quantities appropriately increased (cereal or wholemeal biscuits: very small and small breeds 1½–4 oz, medium breeds

3–4 oz, large 5–8 oz, very large 8–12 oz). For the main meal the quantities of raw meat may be as follows: very small and small breeds 3–7 oz, medium 7–8 oz, large 1–1½ lb, very large breeds 1½–2 lb.

Satisfying a puppy's hunger is important. If he is not satisfied (and sometimes even when he is!) he may well nibble at a chair leg or chew up the corner of a rug. After feeding him, however, the food container should be removed.

It is well to remember also that, when he is fed dry food, he will wish to drink, so his water bowl must be kept filled. Furthermore, after meals the puppy will need wiping off since his muzzle will be messy and his ears – if they are long – may have been dragged through his dinner. Wiping off is best accomplished with a damp cloth.

# INDEX

Acknowledgments

The author and publisher would like to thank the following people
who have helped in the preparation of this book: Anistatia
Vassilopoulos, who designed it; Thomas G. Aylesworth, who
edited it; Cynthia Klein , who prepared the index.

Credits

Animals Unlimited Picture Library, Christina Payne / Paddy
Cutts, kindly provided all of the photographs used in this book.